## CONTENTS

1 Our Story _____ 4

2 Energy _____ 8

3 Emotional _____ 14

4 Physical _____ 21

5 Mental _____ 27

6 Spiritual _____ 31

7 Epilogue _____ 33

Resources _____ 36

www.alexandraaplin.com
Email: alexaplin@mail.com

# Life out of balance completely?

### Do you feel

- Like you can't see a way out?
- Stressed and exhausted?
- Ashamed that your child is behaving aggressively towards you (physically and emotionally)?
- Afraid to take your child to events with family and friends?
- Like you and your family are a square peg in a round hole?
- If you hear "it's behavioural issues" one more time you will go mad?
- Can't take any more conflicting advice?
- Sick of spending tonnes of cash on strategies that don't work?

### This eBook may

- Help you realise that sometimes it's the world that is broken, not you or your child.
- Help you b r e a t h e again.
- Have faith in the future and bring you and your family to HIGHER GROUND
- Watch your child smile again, and maybe even put out the rubbish.

# 1 Our Story

When you think things can't possibly get any worse.

For years I was told by a lot of professionals that my son Luke's issues were caused by my inability to set boundaries. (Turns out this is partly true, however it's not the whole story – sound familiar??) Also that he probably had ODD, that I should just force him to school when he was suicidal, the list goes on.

At the time it seemed that there was not an ounce of compassion coming from anyone.

> Luke was the type of kid who stored up all his stress and anxiety (at school and at his dad's place) and dumped it at home where he felt safe to let it out - you know the story. He struggled to process his emotions and he could be extremely volatile and scary. I knew deep down he wasn't a bad kid, he always showed empathy to his friends and never got into fights at school. Teachers adored him, mostly. I worried that he could end up becoming the "street angel, house devil"

Our journey started early and problems accelerated quickly with the first piece of furniture broken when he was 4. I looked at my tiny baby and wondered where things had gone so drastically wrong. I knew deep down the constant tantrums and drama and constant lack of sleep was more than just behavioural issues. The only way I could contain him at night (that's when most of the problems occurred) would be to strap him into the car and drive up a mountain nearby. I would get him to look up at the stars and out across the city lights. Often it was a soothing distraction. Sometimes it was just too dangerous to drive with him lashing out in the car, so I would have to pull over. This happened so regularly and it would always be at least 11pm before he would settle to sleep. Often much later. I was so completely exhausted all the time (and working full time as a single mum).

So I did what any mother does, I read every parenting book on the planet. Took him to loads of psychologists and psychiatrists yet left with no answers.

I left Luke's father when he was only 1 and the emotional abuse continued for years (for both of us). My mental state became more fragile as did my finances. Anyone in community services will tell you if you support the family they will thrive. That never ever happened. Just a consistent message of

"It's your fault"

Fast forward, years of heartache, years of fighting, years of despair. Finally Luke had a breakdown when he was 12. School refusal led to me losing the small amount of work I had. I became suicidal. I think inheriting a cat saved my life. We were both at rock bottom. I could not see a way out of the hell that our life was. A violent kid at home 24/7, with a broken mumma. Cycle perpetuating.

Around this time, the universe heard my cries for help. Slowly messages came to me that weren't about the "blame game". A very bright lawyer[1] (Mensa member) I met suggested that Luke may be 'gifted'. She asked me about his sleep patterns, his attention levels and a few other things. At the time I never really understood the concept of giftedness. She suggested loads of excellent things like taking him camping, go travelling etc. All things to keep his overactive little brain entertained. I longed to do this, however we were so financially strapped I just went home and cried about it.

A little while later our gorgeous GP suggested he may be on the spectrum, that is, the autism spectrum or maybe gifted. Another GP raised the issue of giftedness, after his school refusal and extreme boredom. During times of extreme volatility - when school refusal started, I ended up resorting to emergency services. Sad but true.

> If you feel in danger of your child call 000, it's the most unnatural thing to do, but it's important to send a message that violence is not acceptable, no matter what the reason or distress behind the outburst.

Most of them were authoritarian and quite frankly afraid. One amazing young police officer (or ambo I can't remember), sat next to me late one night, and with heaps of empathy talked to me about whether Luke was bored at school, highly intelligent, non sleeping etc. He explained all the things a gifted child experiences. I'm so grateful for that hand on my shoulder as I cried on the couch, looking around at all the smashed items in my lounge room.

My thought process changed, I read up on gifted kids and went to heaps of seminars about giftedness. He was ticking every box. These kids often get misdiagnosed with ADHD just because there are so many similarities.

I'm here not only to share our story but to offer you some hope, some reassurance that things can become more peaceful. I don't have a magic wand but I can share some techniques that worked for us. In Dr David Hawkins book Power Vs Force, he says we must share the knowledge we have learnt, if it is to prevent the suffering of others. That is my goal here, I have survived and learnt, and now I hope to share and help you.

If you have felt the sting of the "blame game" as a parent of a child who won't "comply with the rules", I hope this eBook will give you some solace.

1. The lawyer actually linked us into Mensa Kids. It was excellent to meet other parents and highly gifted children. Luke related extremely well with these kids. Water rising to it's own level and all that. After getting an IQ test it was found that he was a little ways off the top 2% required to enter Mensa. It was a great experience though, and the support in this community is amazing. Highly recommend if you feel your kid is in the highly gifted category.

# 2 Energy

## What actually is energy?

Energy, the unseen type is the currency of a quirky kid. Have you ever felt that drain in your stomach (solar plexus) when your child is nagging you? That's energy that you are (sometimes unconsciously) giving out to fuel them.

This will be part of the reason for feeling sooooo damn depleted all the time. Good news is you can transform it, by transforming yourself.

I could actually write a whole book on this subject however, I will just list a few things here that I did to transform this toxic dynamic.

## Nurtured Heart Approach

At a time when I thought that Luke was in such a state that I could absolutely not help him anymore, I chanced upon finding this parenting approach on meetup.com (turns out it's great for grown ups too - and especially those caring for dementia patients & people with mental / intellectual disabilities).

This approach is about creating "inner wealth" in the child - so opposite to many of the traditional parenting approaches. Those techniques I found just want to punish and reward. These kids are way too smart to be treated like pets.

Kids who are labeled ODD often have attachment issues. (Good resource here http://www.attachmentdisordermaryland.com/parenting.htm) When you are wrangling with this type of thing, the kid will fight to the death as though winning is their very survival. It kind of is. For many of us, we know what it feels like to want something you can't have, this is not dissimilar.

The Nurtured Heart Approach (NHA) completely changed our lives. Howard Glasser is the creator of the workbook **"Transforming the Difficult Child"**. It really is a great place to start. I was too exhausted to tackle this alone and I hired a trained NHA consultant for 6 weeks of 1 on 1. Best thing I ever did. I learnt how to change the language I used as a parent and focus on telling Luke about his amazing qualities - and importantly, the benefits of displaying those amazing qualities. *If you think you have not one positive thing to say to your kid right now, don't worry, I felt that way too.*

This approach starts really small. The aim is to build their "portfolio of success" and let go of any disconnecting judgements. The first time I saw this really work was a most extreme experience.

> Luke was about to punch a hole in a stained glass door in absolute frustration. Just before hand and glass connected I said "I know you have control in this moment, I believe you can stop this". His hand stopped.

Of course we were both shocked. In the past I would have screamed something negative like "If you do that you will be in so much trouble". This is exactly the kind of negative energy these kids are used to getting, and they usually crave it and attempt to earn more of it.

> Consequences: How many professionals, teachers or other parents kept up a mantra about "consequences" - It is like a red rag to a bull, for a kid that is already feeling isolated and alienated. With this approach you are just going to drive the problem in deeper & increase their sense of shame.

Over time, using NHA, I finally realised it was working beautifully when Luke actually started craving the positive responses. He would come out and show me awesome things he had done, waiting for the positive feedback. Giving out this type of positive energy is uplifting instead of depletive. I was and still am completely stoked.

## Clear your own trauma

I could also write a whole book on this subject as well, maybe one day I will. You need to be very brave to admit and face that **the world really is our mirror** and we need to do the inner work before it changes. We need to learn that our kids can trigger our own issues that we then project back onto them. They get blamed for all that is wrong with us. Most of us here on Earth have some kind of trauma or even PTSD. Talk therapy, I've found only touches the surface. The "stuff" we carry around in our energy field most definitely **affects our relationships with our kids and others**.

Actually getting that crap out of your energy field will completely change your life and your family dynamic too. How do you do that you ask? Mmm many ways. You will be drawn to the right people at the right time if it's something you are searching for. I will however outline the techniques I've used over the years.

## Institute of Quantum Consciousness

This is similar to hypnosis I guess is the best way I could explain it. A trained practitioner guides you into a relaxed state where you take a particular issue to be resolved. Often the "themes" of the problem will be stemming from an experience that happened early in life (or in past life - if you are into that kind of thing). These experiences create a "charge" or "magnet" that keeps attracting the same experience to you - and they are a request for "resonance".

The last session I experienced uncovered a traumatic event that my subconscious had "created a story" around. That is, I suppressed it because it was just too damn painful to face. I realised this theme had been repeating in my life over and over because that's what happens. The universe will keep delivering these painful experiences time and time again, until we are ready to face them and trash the energy "charge or magnet" once and for all. There it is again, energy. For me it's been the big one.

I loved this technique so much that I completed the facilitator training for the Quantum Consciousness technique in early 2018.

## Narcissistic Abuse Recovery Program - NARP
## (by Melanie Tonia Evans)

Using the NARP approach is where I first found out about the energy charges we carry and **how to clear them**. I always knew about them, but had no idea how to release. Melanie's approach is very comprehensive and almost shamanic. I will be honest, it is quite hard work and very time consuming. It does however get you out of victim consciousness and put you right into an empowered state. Empowered to own your life again.

I first used this technique when going through a custody court case with Luke's father. It transformed all of my fears and traumas so I was finally able to find the truth in the situation. (Instead of dancing around the abuse to pacify the abuser for fear of retribution). I attracted a fabulous female magistrate who cut right to the heart of the situation, and we got Luke's desired outcome. This can be rare in the legal system, which can be expert at protecting the perpetrators at times.

Another huge issue I worked on with the NARP program was dealing with Luke's volatility and inability to contain his aggression and anger. This scared the shit out of me to be honest with you. I thought I had raised a boy who disrespected and would be violent towards women. Little by little I got though this. Not only did I work on my own inner wounds (trauma from violent father/relationships and other abuse), Melanie (the creator of NARP) assisted me in doing some "proxy" healing for Luke. This means you tune into the child (with their soul's permission) and then clear out their wounds without them being physically present. I was lucky enough to have Melanie work with me one on one with this. I highly recommend working with someone first if you decide to do proxy healing, especially if you are new to energy work of this kind. The result of this proxy healing was that I could very quickly see real results, both in Luke and his reactions. He would act out a little at first as he could sense the "energy shift", but then shortly after that there were big changes in his "fight or flight" type responses to stressful stimuli. For the first time in years I didn't have to "be his frontal lobe" for him. He was coming out of the primitive survival brain. (To better understand the biology of trauma read Bessel Van Der Kolk - The Body Keeps the Score).

**Space Clearing**

If you haven't already heard about space clearing, it is also an energetic practice. It's about clearing unseen energies that are discordant. Thought forms or other energies can affect sensitive types. Kids on the spectrum or kids with trauma are often extremely sensitive to these energies or frequencies that are disturbing or negative.

Keeping your house and especially your kids bedroom(s) clear of chaotic energies can really make a difference.

There are many techniques out there; however finding the one that resonates with you is the best. It's often about intention.

Here are a few ways to space clear (find one your kid likes and will tolerate, especially if they have sensory issues). Clean up the area first if you can and then;

- Burning white sage or incense
- Fill a spray bottle with water and 20 drops lavender essential oil - spray all around
- Pray or meditate with intention for all discordant energies/entities to be lifted
- Play music you really love (again with intention to clear). I love using Solfeggio Frequencies (find for free on YouTube)
- Use rescue remedy if you need it

If you feel a very heavy, depressive or scary energy that won't leave, it is time to call in a professional. I have done this a lot as we have moved house a lot. Find a reputable feng shui / geomancy / space clearing consultant in your area. Word of mouth is a good thing.

# 3 Emotional

Highly sensitive and quirky kids can be emotionally messy. Life can be very hard for them, often they feel like they don't quite belong on planet earth. Trying to adapt to a world of conflict and chaos causes much anxiety and also depression and aggression. What goes up must come down. If there is any trauma on top of all that, it will, of course, just exacerbate things.

Being sensitive means that they tune in to everything that is going on around them - and that of course means our own emotional state. This was massive in our situation. Luke was unable to heal emotionally until I started to feel supported and emotionally well also. Children, particularly sensitive children can pick up on vibes, feelings, emotions and energies more than any others.

This ties in a lot with the energy work. We also consulted an amazing homeopathic doctor who worked on possible vaccine damage. Emotions are also affected a lot by diet/leaky gut etc. I will go onto that in the Physical chapter.

**Diagnosis**

First of all I have to say this is not completely necessary and can be quite controversial - as practitioners often get it wrong. Too often parents push for a diagnosis, any diagnosis, any answer and the child is misdiagnosed and in turn their therapies and medication are completely wrong. This is a vicious cycle. My advice would be to follow your intuition on this one. Consult with professionals but listen to your gut and your child first.

One day I found myself hysterically crying at a train station carpark. Nothing was working, I was a wreck, homeless and Luke was acting out in ways that were completely terrifying. After a week of sleeplessness and trauma he jumped head first through a glass sliding door. This was in reaction to a miscommunication with my mum in setting up a TV. I will be honest with you, he lost all control and we were actually afraid that he might hurt one of us. Not long before this he had lashed out and seriously injured my mum's foot. This was all done in "fight / flight" mode. We knew when he wasn't feeling so threatened and afraid, his behaviour was entirely different, but at that time, we had just moved under terrible circumstances, there was a court case going on (custody) and he was feeling increasingly afraid of his father and his reactions. On top of all that I was attempting to manage chronic depression and feelings of shame, which thankfully I have now transformed. At the time I felt I had absolutely no hope in changing the hell that we were experiencing (and my mum as we were living with her).

In this completely gut wrenching moment, I called Behavioural Neurotherapy Clinic in Melbourne. It was a Saturday morning and just by chance the psychologist answered the phone. I was a blubbering and broken mess and so was my child. The psychologist pulled some strings and got us in pronto and bulk billed the lot (the angels were really looking after us on that day). After a load of drama (on his behalf, due to trauma from terrible experiences with "professionals" in the past)[2] we finally got Luke into the clinic for some brain scans and assessments. The results showed over activity in frontal lobe (ADHD) and anxiety disorder. Autism assessment wasn't so cut and dry but it showed that he got a score of 29 when you need 30 to be considered truly "autistic".

Being armed with this information, plus the suggested treatments helped me understand how to manage the situation better (we used Neurofeedback, except couldn't get him to co-operate at the time. Also a big one - diet and supplements). It also opened doors to other supports and education opportunities (like Distance Education). After this I was linked into carer support agencies and respite. Stuff I could have benefitted from over the past 10 years of struggling with my traumatised kid solo. (I actually didn't know I was a "carer", had never really heard the terminology before - coming from a corporate background). If I had any idea what supports were out there, I would have gone through this testing process (challenging as it was) many years ago. So many practitioners just kept sending me home with no support and not a clue what to do next.

The type of support we have received after going through the initially quite gruelling process of applying are:

- A 3 day retreat with other carers staying at a lovely hotel near the ocean.

- A 2 day retreat at an eco resort with other carers and their kids - A carer support worker.

- Access to mental health education plus some additional financial assistance

2. About 6 months prior to this, Luke saw a social worker at our local Child & Adolescent Mental Health Unit. The guy in question was at least 6 foot 7 and enormous. He threatened to assault him, saying he would "come over and break his legs" if he didn't behave. As kids on the spectrum take things very literally this was an incredibly foolish thing to say. I did complain to the hospital director who agreed it was unacceptable. Next time we went to the clinic we were booked in with the very same social worker. I was horrified to say the least.

## Counselling

Luke only responded to one psychologist, **ever**. The only reason for that is because this practitioner got parents in the room with the child. After it ended, he said he only went because he felt he had to. He felt it wasn't successful for him. Talk therapy definitely works for some people, giving them a safe space to vent. However, it wasn't the answer for us.

Research has shown that talk therapy can sometimes re-traumatise people as they are rehashing the painful experiences. There are other techniques to access deeper levels of the brain to process this information effectively. We moved onto therapies that gave us real results, even though that meant going outside the system and spending a lot of money (as these are rarely covered by Medicare).

## Nurtured Heart Approach

Again, back to the NHA. Quite simply it rocks, and we still use it to this day. Luke now even uses it on me, frequently highlighting my qualities rather than just constantly telling me how "crap" I am as a mother.

Other Emotional Trauma Treatments we have used:

**EMDR/Brainspotting** - Personally, I think it worked brilliantly in shifting some long held trauma. This is achieved by shifting neuro pathways in the brain to release associated feelings to trauma. For me I could feel a physical release of the trauma we were working on using EMDR. This is a technique where the practitioner gets you to think about a traumatic event and then directs you to move your eyes left to right. This helps you go into your subconscious program to find out where the problems are.

From **https://www.brucelipton.com/resource/article/epigenetics**

Dr Lipton's research suggests that the subconscious mind is built on habituation. It learns from patterns and repetition of patterns. By accessing that invisible field, you can rewrite those habits. The million-dollar question is, how? According to Dr. Lipton, we can do this in many ways. "Through processes such as hypnosis, subliminal tapes, the religious use of affirmations, Buddhist mindfulness, or a series of reprogramming modalities collectively referred to as energy psychology....including EMDR and Emotional Freedom Technique (EFT) among many other new techniques we can rewrite those destructive programs that occupy our subconscious field.

**Quantum Consciousness** - see in Energy chapter

## Neurofeedback

This cost a lot of money for us at the time. I was unable to get Luke to engage with this treatment either. I tried it myself and found it really really exhausting, but we were only using a home PC version (traditional or Brainwave Neurofeedback). I ended up researching this extensively as I have TBI (traumatic brain injury - discovered after a QEEG brain scan). There seems to be many amazing types of neurofeedback out there, however it is all incredibly expensive and I was unable to find it all in Melbourne. After the fact I found out that Behavioural Neurotherapy Centre generally use two types of neurofeedback at once for most effective results. They only offered me the traditional type as they knew I was unable to use the much more expensive in-clinic treatments. I was pretty annoyed about that. Would have been good to know this upfront. I really recommend reading **The Neurofeedback Solution by Stephen Larsen**. Was very inspiring and if you have time and money it could be an extremely valuable treatment.

Neurofeedback is brain retraining using the concept of neuroplasticity. The Brainwave type we used involved putting on a very sexy cap on your brain, which has electrodes (19 channels) on it. You are then hooked up to a machine which monitors your brain activity. You generally are doing a repetitive activity in the way of a game which has been designed especially for your brain ie increasing alpha activity for example). My brain scan showed overactivity in frontal lobe (ADHD) and under activity in other areas. There are some newer and more advanced styles of neurofeedback and they use other techniques. These include:

- 3D Neurofeedback - (QEEG Z-score LoRETA - real time)
- Low Energy Neurofeedback (LENS)
- NeuroField Pulsed Electromagnetic Frequency
- Meditating monks and nuns who pray have had brain scans. It has been proven that these techniques also "mould" or train the brain. Food for thought.

**Music**

The effects of music on the brain are well known to be beneficial.

> The French Doctor Alfred Tomatis devised a listening system that allowed sufferers to develop differentiated brain maps by training their hearing. One of the troubled young men he helped, Paul Madaule, went on to create a listening therapy – based on music and the mother's voice – for children with learning difficulties. According to Doidge (Norman Doige author The Brain's Way of Healing), the effects have been extraordinary.

During possibly the worst period of Luke's life, he was unreachable, volatile, withdrawn and completely traumatised. Expensive items in the house were getting smashed regularly. We really were at our wits end. I was terrified every day when I woke up, wondering how I would duck and weave through this war zone. I worried for all of our own safety, I worried about his future and I wondered if any of it was going to end. I was full of shame, regret, anger and serious feelings of loneliness and isolation.

I soldiered on and had just finished reading The Brain's Way of Healing and decided to give the music with mother's voice trick a go. With the help of my mum, we recorded some soft music (pretty sure it was Solfeggio), with my voice over the top. I was saying positive affirmations like "you are safe and calm", "today is going to be wonderful" etc. We waited till Luke was asleep and played this very softly in his room. The results were very positive and we noticed a sense of calmness starting to show up in his demeanour. Trying to match up with his sleep disordered times of rest was the challenge but we managed occasionally. My mum has told me this technique is called **"Sleep Talk"**. We just used the mother's voice and the music, and added the Nurtured Heart Approach, so it was a bit of a "cocktail" of treatments, with pretty good results.

# 4 Physical

Possibly most important and probably most challenging.
From the get go, I attempted to get Luke on my page with regard to physical health, sport, diet, yoga (I'm a teacher) and supplements etc etc. It would have worked really well to create rituals around these things from a young age. Sadly I didn't have the awareness then that I have now.

Any time I attempted to implement dietary changes, I was met with a war. Brain gym - opposition. Homeopathy - scorn and disbelief. On occasion I got some level of cooperation but overall it was a battle of the wills. Too smart and too afraid to actually heal. I discovered the concept of Secondary Gain a while ago which explains this fear to get well. Happens to all of us. Often we keep the status quo of a negative situation, because we are actually getting something out of it. I read an article about this, where a woman with cancer would not heal, as she was getting love and attention from her husband. He normally was absent and cold.

These are things I have found to be highly effective. It doesn't however mean that my child has stuck with it. On the contrary I'm usually met with opposition. Intellectually about 23, emotionally 3 some days, 11 other days.

**Diet**

We all know diet is important regardless of age and that children should have a nice clean diet. For years I knew about the gut/brain axis, however I didn't really take it seriously. The GAPS Diet and Gut Healing Protocol are things I have looked into lately (mainly for myself). The first time I managed to get Luke to change his diet, miraculous things happened in the house.

He was less hyperactive, less volatile and he ACTUALLY WENT TO SLEEP AT A NORMAL TIME (this had not happened since he was 3).

The diet was prescribed by a naturopath who is renowned in Melbourne. His name is Jim O'Hearn. It was basically a ketogenic diet with high quality yoghurt being the only dairy (sugar free like Jalna). The first 2 weeks of the diet were stricter, including minimal fruit and allium (garlic /onion). Rice was allowed but only if you toasted it first in a fry pan (then steam or boil as usual). This is because it changes the carbohydrate component.

It was pretty stressful sending Luke to school with tuna or chicken salad (for him not me), but seeing the incredible changes, I soldiered on. After a few weeks he just lost it, the war zone started again. The other thing that was probably occurring was withdrawal. Dairy protein and gluten etc are highly addictive like opiates, so I may have made him go "cold turkey". I realise this now, but wasn't aware at the time. Since then I try with moderate success to get him to eat a whole food diet at a minimum. It's successful sometimes, but not enough for my liking. He had a consult with an holistic GP. Tested off the charts for HPL (also known as Mauve Factor or kryptopyrolle) and low in iron and zinc.

Individuals with high-Mauve cannot efficiently create serotonin – and are pretty much always deficient in zinc and B6. This article from Joe Cohen's Selfhacked explains https://selfhacked.com/blog/everything-know-high-mauve/

Basically if you can cut out artificial flavours and colours, gluten and at least low sugar & carbohydrates, that is a great place to start. Getting advice off a regarded health professional is an excellent idea. Lots of conflicting advice right now but follow your intuition on this.

## Medication

I chose not to medicate when Luke was young. When things got very bad for us, not one health professional would prescribe medication (not even melatonin). At the time we needed it the most due to severe sleep disorder/anxiety. Go figure. During a trip to emergency after a huge and spectacular meltdown, the GP gave us some valium to take home. I was completely exhausted after the circus at ER, and my mum sat with him during the night while he hallucinated, calmly apparently, but in another dimension all the same. Since that experience he refuses medication of any type. Fair call I thought, even though there were times when I felt like shoving it into his Milo.

About 12 months ago we found CBD Hemp Oil to be very helpful for anxiety/depression. After hearing the recommendation several times in a short space of time, I took the hint from the universe. (Choose carefully with this product as there are so many out there, with differing concentrations.) We purchase ours from Kevin at Shamanic Rain:

https://www.shamanicrain.com.au

It has been proven to be highly effective with returned soldiers with PTSD. I often joked with Luke that he was like Leuitenant Dan (from Forrest Gump) as they both displayed similar rage, volatility, addiction and disconnection commonly present in PTSD.

Slowly, after he started taking the highly concentrated dose, there were little moments of fantastic and clear communication from him. Instead of throwing his dinner across the floor in a rage because he didn't like the flavour or texture he said things like this:

> "Mum I know you like your meat cooked well done, but I really like mine rare. Can you cook it like that next time? I can't help it, I just don't like it cooked too much, it's too chewy"

I was in shock. It was the first time I had heard my kid negotiate. More and more he started to calmly express his needs. Soon after this he also started to talk to me about his distress about missing his half sister and also how challenging it had been staying at his dad's house every other weekend. (It was nearly 3 years since the court case ended and I was given full custody of Luke. After this he has never seen his half sister or any other extended family on that side).

He would regularly come home on a Sunday night (after weekend dad visits) and just explode. He explained to me that he felt like "a pile of dried leaves" and that all he needed was a tiny little spark for it to all become a firestorm.

Luke acknowledged that it was rarely my fault, but it was just that he felt unable to express himself at his dad's house, therefore he felt like he had to hold in all his feelings. (On top of that he could never sleep - and actually had to lie there pretending to be asleep because he was too scared to get up).

**Blue light / EMF / Wi-Fi radiation**

This is such a massive issue in our times. I wish it was something easily controllable but it's certainly not. Electrosmog in the world and in our homes is increasingly growing. Radiation from our devices should be alarming us, but in our connected world we see little babies holding mobile phones to their heads. The rollout of 5G mobile is alarming many as it uses untested higher frequencies. What's it doing to us? There are many studies showing that EMF reduction can assist in healing our bodies and minds. Professor Charlie Teo (famous Australian Brain Cancer Surgeon) recommends using mobile phones hands free and keeping devices at the foot of the bed. He also suggests turning off electric blankets when sleeping and waiting for the microwave to beep before opening.

In France , Wi-Fi is banned in nursery schools and wifi routers are turned off in primary schools when not in use. Should we all be doing the same? One thing I know is that whenever I have taken Luke camping, HE IS COMPLETELY DIFFERENT. He sleeps easily, is more relaxed and more sociable to name a few things. I also notice changes in myself too. My health is always better and I just "feel" better. Turning Wi-Fi off at night for at least 12 hours is a great place to start. I've also heard that low emission mobile phones will soon be available. Apart from that, trying to keep ourselves connected to the Earth[3], more than our devices has got to be a good thing.  Trying to get iGen to participate, that's the tricky part.

3. The quickest and easiest way to get a better connection to the earth I've found, is getting my bare feet on the ground as much as possible. Dr Patrick Flanagan says this is the best and cheapest medicine available to humanity as we are absorbing Earth's healing energy. You must have bare feet though directly on the ground (no concrete). Indigenous cultures also talk about this method as well for healing. Find out more about Dr Flanagan here https://www.gaia.com/person/patrick-flanagan

Blue light from screens disrupts the bodies natural circadian rhythms. When Luke had the "breakdown" half way through grade 6, he curled up in a ball, wrapped himself in a blanket and glued himself to the screen. He was self medicating, with comedies on YouTube. Apart from being highly addictive, all this exposure to blue light had devastating effects on his sleep patterns. (Of course emotional trauma didn't help). Since then I've attempted to get him to use blue light blocking apps or glasses. It hasn't been successful, I hope he will one day understand how much this affects his brain/life.

## Body Movement / Body Awareness

This is powerful and often forgotten.

> "Trauma Victims cannot recover until they become familiar with, and befriend the sensations in their bodies. Being frightened means that you live in a body that is always on guard"
> BESSEL VAN DER KOLK, The Body Keeps the Score

If your child is into sport, dance or similar this is fantastic. Luke has had a love/hate relationship with sport. I've done everything in my power to keep body movement happening in his world. It's not always easy. The one thing I noticed that worked amazingly was martial arts for him. He started Tae Kwon Do and soon after that he started sleeping better and his cognition seemed a lot better. Unfortunately his friend quit so he did as well. The discipline wasn't something he could get used to either.

Moving trauma out of the body can be done in many ways. Swimming, dance, yoga, tai chi, sport etc. A technique I have discovered lately is called TRE - Trauma Release Exercise. It's also used frequently on returned service men and women with PTSD. More details here http://treaustralia.com.au/

# 5 Mental

## Getting Enough Stimulation

If your child is gifted or has high functioning autism or ADHD (apparently, all of this is on a spectrum of some kind), not much will prepare you for the journey you will be embarking on. It's safe to say that a load of people, including family and friends, will have no clue what your life is like and in many regards even if they have experienced it, their journey will be different. I have found on this journey of mine, every situation is completely unique.

From a young age, Luke has been intellectually advanced. The only reason I knew this is because others told me. Caregivers at creche, friends who were teachers and sometimes family. I kind of brushed it off, because in our culture, telling everyone your child is beyond his years is considered arrogant, or in the country where I grew up, just plain up yourself.

If I had more of a clue about this fact when the young man was 2 and showing signs of hyperactivity I would have had a better understanding of his needs. Boredom to these kids is literally worse than death. Utterly EXHAUSTING to parents, however if you find a lot of ways to keep mental stimulation happening it will mean a happier kid. Tough call if finances are strained, however utilising local libraries and toy libraries can be an excellent resource when kids are little.

Luke also found his own ways to process the inner turbulence he was feeling, through his own play therapy. Gifted and creative kids often do. He would often engage others into his games, however you would soon find yourself being booted out if you didn't follow the rules. I highly recommend allowing this process even if it is annoying or unconventional.

Here are some ways Luke unravelled his own trauma through play:

- Lining up all of his matchbox cars in a "race". Wooden spoons, shoes etc became the pits. The race could go on for days actually, and if it was disturbed he would be incredibly distressed. His tendency to be obsessive showed up in these situations, like Sheldon and his chair in "The Big Bang Theory". He used sound and motion making a real Formula 1 race track in the lounge room. He would always make sure one of the cars was for his half sister (who he missed and loved greatly).

- Turning the couch upside down to become a boat. I was once fired for having narcolepsy as a deck hand, my mum reminded me (she was hired too, but was a more reliable crew mate)

- His baby stuffed animals were in little pairs and families. These were played with on the floor and set up in bed every night - all in a certain order of course. We were evacuated during Black Saturday bushfires and when I found Luke's suitcase at the door, the little baby animal heads were popping out of the front zip. Inside the suitcase the clothes had been discarded and replaced was a fluffy blanket and one of the larger animals. I ignored the clothes at that point and realised these things were of greater importance to him.

These types of games I think were invaluable for him as he was unable to verbalise any pain he was experiencing.

Some of our favourite free or inexpensive activities now are;

- Movies (I have a Companion Card for Luke so we get him in for free - a psychologist helped me with the application). Other things we have done using Companion Card are Monster Trucks, Comedy Festival, museums, Scienceworks, PAX and Supanova (like Comic-Con)

- A lot of free lectures - particularly at Swinburne University which has excellent talks on Astronomy. Found this on meetup.com via an Astronomy Group.

- Royal Society of Victoria have many excellent talks and activities for science nuts. They have connections with RMIT and John Monash High School

- meetup.com is excellent for things like Nerf Gun War meetings and games of all kinds. (I don't have a girl, so sorry this is all "boyish")

- Boarding down sand dunes at Kilcunda, anything outdoors that is high energy

**Appropriate Education**

This is probably the most challenging thing if you have a gifted or highly gifted child. An organisation that helped me a lot with this initially is **Born to Soar.** These guys fill the gap for bright kids in their usual school environment. It of course only works if your child is engaged in school in the first place. Mine had given up by then. Years ago state schools actually catered for these kids, but due to funding cuts they now often fall through the cracks. In the case of Luke, extreme boredom was a contributor to his breakdown. As mentioned earlier for gifted or ADHD kids boredom can be worse than death. I was diagnosed with ADHD when I was 42, and I can attest to that. I don't cope with boredom very well at all.

After the school refusal went on for 6 months I realised something had to give. Homeschooling and unschooling has helped us a lot with this. It took a year for both of us to "deschool". This is the rewiring in your brain required to change a lifetime of education habits (or brainwashing by "the system" if you prefer).

Unschooling or self directed learning helped Luke overcome the boredom at school. The curriculum was mind numbing for him. I could not afford specialist schools so this was our solution. I've had to change my entire way of being as well, by working primarily from home. This is not for the feint hearted that's for sure. Initially I thought spending 24/7 with this tsunami of a child would kill me. We evolved and adapted and now it is our way of life. A move away from the masses has its benefits. Traveling outside school holidays, going to special events on school days. For a kid who doesn't cope with crowds this is actually a huge bonus. There are many excellent resources on unschooling and homeschooling.

- Support groups on Facebook dedicated to both homeschooling and unschooling.
- Blake Boles, **http://www.blakeboles.com/**
- John Holt who penned the term "Unschooling" **https://www.johnholtgws.com**
- The Educating Parent **http://homeschoolaustralia.com**
- Gifted Homeschoolers **https://giftedhomeschoolers.org**

# 6 Spiritual

Kids are naturally spiritual. They don't question things we have been conditioned to "squash". Luke is incredibly psychic, as are many kids. He often saw entities when he was little, and spoke about it. He doesn't speak about these things anymore, but tells me he sees colours around things and people. Auras.

Growing up with a yoga teacher for a mum, he has been exposed to yoga, meditation and qigong from the get go. I used to play a particular piece of music to meditate to when I was pregnant. I never forget one day, when he was around 2, he sat perfectly still next to the fire with his hands upturned on his lap. He sat like this for quite a while. We were all stunned as he was normally pretty hyperactive. I realised then, that exact same piece of music was playing that I used for meditation while pregnant. Pretty amazing display of neuroplasticity.

I didn't intentionally try to push my beliefs onto Luke, he usually opposes most things anyway. I did however, let him use the tools "of my trade" when he needed them. He followed the yoga poses until it was no longer "cool" (aged 4). He secretly loves it when I use the pendulum to dowse for him (to find answers to his problems or concerns). He's not confident enough yet to use himself, but you never know one day. I've bought him crystals, and let him choose his own. He carries them everywhere, but wouldn't dare tell his mates. All this from a boy who claims to be staunchly scientific and even had a stand up screaming match with the pastor at school. They were arguing about evolution vs creationism. He was 9. He chose to sit it out in the library during RE (this is in a public school, I'm not sure if they still have religious education anymore).

Feeling gratitude is also something I speak about with Luke. We attempted Heart Math **https://www.heartmath.com** when he was 7 or 8 - at a very difficult time. It's about feeling love or gratitude as you breathe and consciously focus on your heart. This is scientifically proven to "smooth" your heart rate variable (HRV). If your HRV is messy and jagged it's a sign you are tense and stressed. This affects the electrical field around your body - which is emanating from your heart. This is measured with a little gadget attached to iPhone / app. It's very powerful and uplifting.

I have always encouraged the importance of finding your joy and your purpose. This wasn't encouraged when I was a kid in our family. I have always made it clear that friends and family are super important and that a sense of community is a blessing and so critical to success (both individually and for humanity). Man is not an island and all that. "Breaking bread" with others is an important spiritual activity. This is something I have always encouraged as well. Sharing meals with others. There is something about bonding with others over a meal. This hasn't always been easy, as poverty caused a lot of moving and instability, making it very challenging to form lasting relationships and even afford to share food (as sometimes we could hardly afford it for ourselves). I just hope that the guidance I have tried to impart has had some kind of lasting affect. Each day I see positive changes in Luke, so I feel that it "soaked into" him somehow. All the times I thought that the hell was never going to end, I'm here to say that it can. With determination, hope, patience, work and **love** you can do anything.

# 7 Epilogue

**Where are things now you ask?**

Well as always in these situations, nothing is completely perfect. I can say though, that there is greater peace, communication and feeling of, well, possibility. Luke suffers with social anxiety and definitely has a screen addiction. I was berated for suggesting the latter on a homeschool forum. Two mums, who were themselves autistic, trolled me for saying he had a screen addiction, but I should actually consider that, this could be the only way he felt safe relating to the world. Autism and trauma can make you feel incredibly unsafe. If you have seen the series **Atypical** or **The Good Doctor,** this explains why.

The custody court case was about Luke's desire to no longer see his dad on alternate weekends. The magistrate granted his wish. After years of mediation and legal wrangling the stress of that situation ended. Of course it was bittersweet, because all he really wanted was for his dad to show some, any, kind of empathy or compassion. Luke truly loves his dad and his extended family, but he lost the whole lot in one fell swoop, or rather they gave up on him it seems. The upshot is that the space this created for Luke to heal his trauma has been so needed. Before the court case everything seemed impossible, like there was never a space for releasing the pain. Just a constant "re-opening" of the wounds. Always feeling a little bit like an "orphan" myself due to my wanderlust, I have always created my own family wherever I go. This is something Luke is finally starting to do. He's befriended a local homeschool kid, who is also on the spectrum. They have a lot in common and have become quite close over the last few months in particular. Some of the other guys in his strategy board games group have invited him to hang out with them. In the last six months Luke has started planning and talking about his future. A year ago that never would have happened. He is also sharing with me a lot of the complex ideas in his head, often about politics and how to make the world a better place.

He's still afraid of going to uni, even though aerospace engineering is his passion (Formula 1 Racing). I constantly let him know that nothing is impossible and we will find a way to make it happen. Of course he needs to actually find his way to settling some of the anxiety, or pushing through the pain and doing it anyway. Temple Grandin is famous for saying to parents of kids on the spectrum to challenge them and find ways to help them stay connected to the world. Temple is on the autism spectrum and has written many fantastic books on the subject. **http://www.templegrandin.com/**

This journey has utterly changed my life in so many ways. In attempting to heal my son, I have healed myself. I've obtained greater awareness and understanding, and found that I am also traumatised and have neurological issues. When Luke had a brain scan at age 12 I decided it would be good if I had one too, mainly because I could finally see that the attention deficits he had, I also had too. I'm probably on the autism spectrum too, but I didn't have the test. (Autism often shows up very differently in girls/women too, as we are more adept at communication/networking - generally anyway). When I was a child these symptoms were hardly recognised and offered ignored. My coping skills up till age 30 included wagging school, self medicating with sugar, caffeine, alcohol, sex and for a short time drugs. I managed to outsource tasks that I found excruciatingly boring, either by paying for it, or using guile, wit and charm. When I could no longer use these destructive tools to cope, I was forced to find new, healthy ways of being. I have cleared a lot of the trauma held in my body and feel like I am not stuck in a holding pattern anymore. Kind of like thriving versus surviving.

Like you, we will continue to grow, learn and evolve. I hope that these tools help you as much as they have helped us.

# Resources

**Mensa Kids Australia**

https://www.mensa.org.au/giftedchildren/gifted-children

**Nurtured Heart Approach**

https://childrenssuccessfoundation.com

**In Melbourne** http://www.caringwithheart.com.au/

**Transforming the Difficult Child Workbook**

https://www.amazon.com/Transforming-Difficult-Child-Nurtured-Approach/dp/0967050707

**Meetup**

meetup.com

**Born to Soar**

https://www.borntosoar.com.au

**Excellent info on Oppositional Defiance Disorder**

http://www.attachmentdisordermaryland.com/parenting.htm

**Institute of Quantum Consciousness**

http://www.instituteforquantumconsciousness.com

**Narcissistic Abuse Recovery Program - Melanie Tonia Evans**

https://www.melanietoniaevans.com

**The Body Keeps the Score by Bessel Van Der Kolk**

http://www.traumacenter.org/products/Amazon_staff_books.php

**The Neurofeedback Solution by Stephen Larsen**

http://stonemountaincenter.com/site/the-neurofeedback-solution/

**The Brain's Way of Healing - Norman Doige**

http://www.normandoidge.com

**Joe Cohen's Self Hacked**

https://selfhacked.com

**Dr Patrick Flanagan**

https://www.gaia.com/person/patrick-flanagan

**TRE - Trauma Release Exercise**

http://treaustralia.com.au

**EMDR - Eye Movement Desensitising & Repatterning**

http://emdraa.org

**Companion Card**

http://www.companioncard.org.au

**Supanova - Comic Con & Gaming**

http://www.supanova.com.au

**Royal Society of Victoria - Science Promotion / events**

https://rsv.org.au

**Atypical TV Series**

https://www.netflix.com/title/80117540

www.ingramcontent.com/pod-product-compliance
Lightning Source LLC
Chambersburg PA
CBHW032053290426
44110CB00012B/1069